How to deal with Power and Manipulation

by Performance Consulting

Nigel Harrison

performance consulting : uk

Published in 2014

Performance Consulting UK Ltd
32 Victoria Road
Sheffield
S10 2DL

© Nigel Harrison, 2014

ISBN: 978-0-9559068-1-7

Layout and graphics by Jonathan Horner [email@jonhorner.co.uk]

Proof editing by Annette Waterhouse [annette.waterhouse@bigfoot.com]

Printed and bound by CPI Group (UK) Ltd, Croydon, CR0 4YY

How to deal with Power and Manipulation by Performance Consulting

Nigel Harrison

performance consulting : uk

What to do when a rational approach does not work and you need to deal with:

- **INNOCENT MANIPULATION**
- **POWERFUL NEGOTIATION**
- **DELIBERATE MANIPULATION**

Contents

Who is this book for?

- Performance Consultants
- Business Partners
- Learning and Development Partners
- H.R. Business Partners
- I.T. Consultants
- Financial Consultants
- Executives and Leaders

About the author

Nigel Harrison is a Chartered Business Psychologist, Performance Consultant and author of *Improving Employee Performance* and *How to be a True Business Partner by Performance Consulting*.

For the last 25 years he has been helping internal consultants and managers to adopt a 7-step performance consulting process to find solutions to any problem. **HOWEVER**, when they return to work many people struggle to cope with the irrational world of power and manipulation.

The ideas and opinions in this book are based on the real experiences of internal consultants coming to terms with real managers and leaders. It is not a theoretical or rigorous study but based on the experience of internal consultants, shared in our advanced workshops, where we investigate the barriers within the organisation to rational performance consulting. The content is meant to be challenging and opinionated, to try to get close to the reality that many of us experience.

What is written here is not "true". You need to relate these ideas to your own experience, decide what works for you, try the ideas out in reality and determine what is "true" for you. Good luck!

Nigel Harrison
nigel @performconsult.co.uk

This book is a sequel to *How to be a True Business Partner by Performance Consulting*, a rational approach to solving performance problems in partnership with our clients. Notice the collaborative words: "**True**" and "**Partner**". This approach works in most cases but does depend on having a client who is prepared to face up to the real issues.

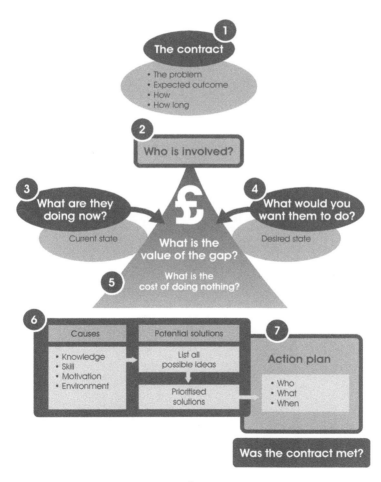

2 When a rational approach doesn't work

What happens when the client is **resistant** to working in partnership and wants to use their **power** to avoid facing up to the problem and to get you to do what they want?

People such as:

- *The H.R. Director who tells his Learning Manager "You just don't understand that I want you to do as you are told!"*
- *The Sales Director who says "We need more sales coaching. I have agreed a budget with the executive – just get it organised."*
- *The H.R. Director who pushes all L&D (Learning and Development) solutions from an H.R. perspective, using fashionable buzzwords and generalisations such as "leadership".*

In some way these people are manipulating others.

How do you know when you are being manipulated?

Most of the time, people respond in a rational, kind and agreeable way. However, occasionally things do not feel right and we **feel upset, unsure** and **uncomfortable**. In these cases, you may be being manipulated by others. Are your feelings telling you something but you are not sure what the problem is? The rational facts and words that people are using make sense at one level but you **feel** that something is wrong, and you may end up taking on projects:

- That you feel uncertain about
- That you have been asked not to question
- That you will have to work very hard to deliver to a deadline
- Where you will be blamed if things go wrong
- Where you do not have access to the resources you need to complete the task
- Where you have been given the impression that you need to prove your competence to deliver.

Apart from our early family life, we choose who we interact with, **except** the people we meet at work.

Our interactions at work are further complicated by the fact that people have power over us. Our boss may control our performance review, ratings, bonus, information and promotion prospects. "Senior" people in the organisation literally have a higher grade than us and influence over what we should do.

In these situations there is potential for manipulation, both innocent and deliberate, and we need to know how to deal with it.

Power and its abuse is all around us, and when you end up doing something for someone else that may not be to your benefit, or the benefit of the organisation, then I think you are being manipulated.

Different types of manipulation

In this book I suggest three levels of manipulation and three different strategies for coping with it:

- Innocent manipulation
- Powerful resistance
- Deliberate manipulation.

I have modified the performance consulting process to show how we make decisions based on what sort of reaction we are getting from our clients.

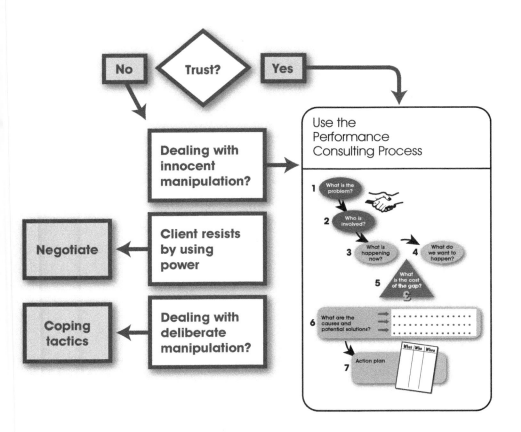

When you deal with manipulation, what type is it?

I asked several of my clients and the consensus was:

Innocent manipulation	**90%**
Powerful resistance	**7%**
Deliberate manipulation	**3%**

We all thought that the biggest thing you have to deal with is clients who are too busy, too stressed to face up to the real problem and therefore jump to "solutioneering" and innocent manipulation as the easy way out.

These are the sort of clients who have already decided that training is the solution and want you to take the order. They try to manipulate you by presenting the order as a "fait accompli", by rushing you and not listening to your questions if you challenge their simplistic view of the world and their solution.

So keep this in mind as you read this book. Most people you meet will be innocent manipulators, and as long as you are authentic you can use the performance consulting approach to work with them and help them to face up to the real problems.

What is power?

Can you remember a time when:

- You clearly felt that someone was using power against you?
- You clearly exercised power over an individual or group?

Take a minute to reflect on a situation like this, and the how the experience felt.

In both cases I am sure that you have a clear idea of what power meant **but** one of the reasons that power is still the *"last dirty secret of the organisation"* is the difficulty of defining it as a concept. Charles Handy made a valiant attempt:

Power = influence – A's ability to modify B's attitude or behaviour.

French and Raven categorised different sorts of power:

PHYSICAL POWER	A is bigger, stronger, more beautiful than B
RESOURCE	A controls reward which must be desired by B
POSITION	A has authority via role
CONTROL	A has assets and right of access to influence stakeholders
EXPERT	Information and expertise that are valued (information is power)
CHARISMA	Self confidence (increased by position and office)

In addition power can be:

LEGITIMATE	Agreed by consensus
NEGATIVE	e.g. Deletion and distortion of information. Delaying or not completing agreed actions (increases with low morale)

Within this power can also be:

OVERT	Force, persuasion, rules and procedures
COVERT	Culture, design of work, reward systems, "The way things work around here"
PERSONAL	Expertise, competence, charisma, attraction, trust, loyalty

The results of exercising power can be:

COMPLIANCE	Needs energy to maintain
INTERNALISED	Adopts as own idea Induction, apprenticeship, brain washing, socialisation e.g. military initial training schemes

In really simplistic terms ...

Powerful and nice might be:

Competent, trusted leader with self-confidence, who builds personal loyalty and an effective culture and reward system so that the way we do things around here builds other people's confidence to do the right things for the benefit of everyone.

The values and behaviours are internalised so individuals internalise the beliefs and behaviour as their own.

Powerful and manipulative might be:

Physically imposing leader with formal authority who uses force, persuasion, rules and procedures to gain compliance which needs continual energy to maintain.

Very little research has been done on organisational power

One reason is that the concept can be over-used or used loosely to describe so many things:

> *The power of the Trade Unions* – Is this legitimate power or negative power?
>
> *The power of celebrity* – Is this personal or positional power or both?

Love is a similarly broad concept. The success of *Les Miserables* has been ascribed to its multiple themes of love – parental, romantic, unrequited and brotherly. Power and love are similarly vague concepts. Bertrand Russell described power as the fundamental stuff of human relationships in a way that energy is the fundamental concept in physics.

Your concept of power can depend on your political view and if you have been relatively successful in life it will be a lot less apparent to you than if you have not.

The subjective nature of the concept is one of the reasons why researchers do not investigate power in organisations.

Power is totally subjective but we all know about it.

On a scale of 1–10 rate how powerful you are compared with:

a) Your boss.

b) A colleague.

c) A subordinate.

	1	2	3	4	5	6	7	8	9	10
a										
b										
c										

I bet you can do it quite easily.

Power, the last guilty secret of the organisation

Does talking about power and manipulation make you uncomfortable? Do you think that nothing like that could happen in your organisation? Several of my clients have this reaction until they start to think about their clients who insist on solutions that don't make sense, and then use power to push through their solution.

> *"Yes, we thought it was funny at the time when they insisted we train their staff when we could see no benefit."*

Power has been called the last guilty secret of the organisation. Psychologists and managers have been reluctant to admit to and tackle the use of power and manipulation in organisations, preferring instead a rational view of the world. For the last twenty years, I have been training internal consultants in performance consulting and I did not fully appreciate the power of irrational forces (especially "solutioneering") that you have to face.

The first thing we need to do is admit to and recognise that there is a power-ridden and irrational side to any organisation. This is the opposite of what the organisation is trying to project to the world through its structures, job titles, etc. As well as the rational side of any organisation, there is the "other side", involving the use of power and of emotional, instinctive and "quick fix" decision-making by normal people under pressure.

The great solutions conspiracy

Much of the misuse of power I see in my clients' worlds is caused by our human tendency to jump to solutions too quickly. Our clients often approach us in an agitated state asking for instant solutions, for example:

> *"They need sales training. Can you get it organised by June. I have the budget agreed by the exec."*

At first sight this seems reasonable, but notice the language in the problem statement:

"They" – the client has already decided who the target group for learning solutions are.

"need sales training" – they have selected the solution and method and expect this to solve the complex performance problem on its own.

"you get it organised" – you are now responsible for implementing the solution with no further involvement from themselves – you are a "pair of hands" not a "trusted advisor".

"I have had the budget agreed by the exec" – I am more powerful than you.

"by June" – I have made a commitment for delivery which I expect you to keep for me.

Such a simple statement reflects how this Learning and Development person is regarded by their clients. It could reflect deliberate domination and manipulation, or it could be innocent "solutioneering".

The statement could also be a challenge to see how an L&D Consultant reacts.

If they react as an "order taker":

> **Inner dialogue:** *"Great — someone needs me and they have a budget for an interesting L&D solution."*

Or:

> **Inner dialogue:** *"How are we going to get this done by June? Have we got enough sales expertise to run this? What do I know about suitable courses?"*

In both cases, the L&D person has accepted the order at face value and is living within their own head (thinking inside their own box), and working in a superficial way. If they accept the order at face value, they will have missed the opportunity to engage with this client at a deeper level of credibility and intimacy. They will also have colluded in a fantasy (the great training conspiracy).

The Training Conspiracy

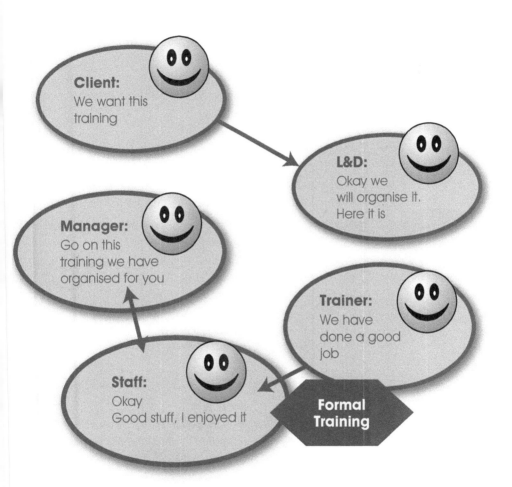

When a Rational Approach Doesn't Work

You will notice that:

- This is a "closed loop" system.
- Everyone is happy within this system.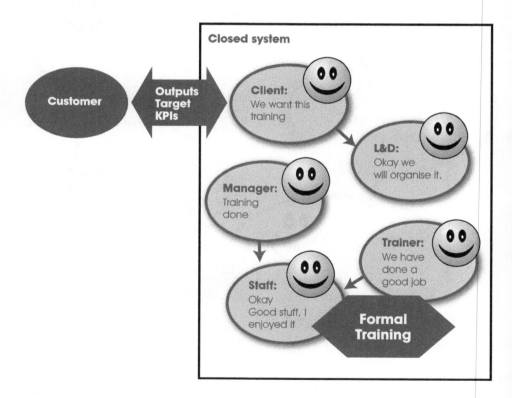
- No one is challenged.
- There is no link to the real business problem.
- The supplier has not entered the "red-zone" of the clients, outputs, targets, KPIs (Key Performance Indicators).

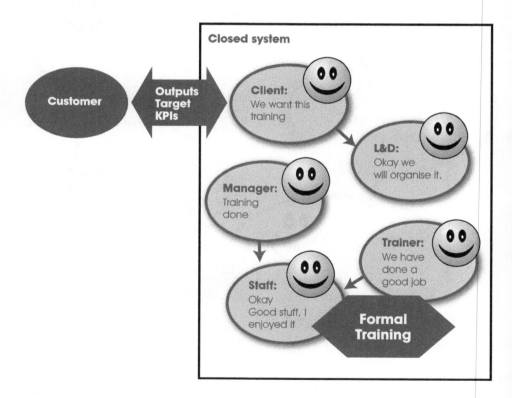

This "closed loop system" can maintain itself because no one is getting the negative feedback that would force a change.

The closed system has traditionally also limited the methods of learning to formal learning that we can control within the system.

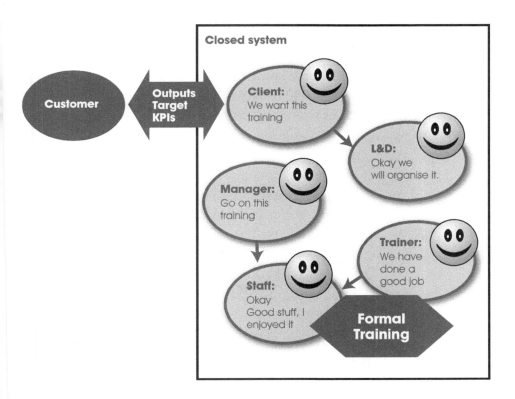

This has been challenged recently by the work on 70:20:10 Learning Formula, which stresses the importance of informal learning as it contributes up to 70% of what we actually learn.

A dysfunctional system

Radio 4 reported on car accident insurance scams and said that everyone in the system was behaving badly. One group changing its behaviour would not solve the problem because *"in a dysfunctional system everyone behaves in a dysfunctional way"*. I think it is the same in the Training Conspiracy. It's not deliberate but a dysfunctional system has evolved:

- Senior Managers think they know the Training solutions and do not get challenged on their real performance problems.
- Training Managers get interesting projects.
- Trainers deliver brilliant solutions.
- Learners enjoy the experience.

So what's not to like? But it is a **closed system**, not connected to the business problem and, because it has benefits for all involved, it is self-perpetuating.

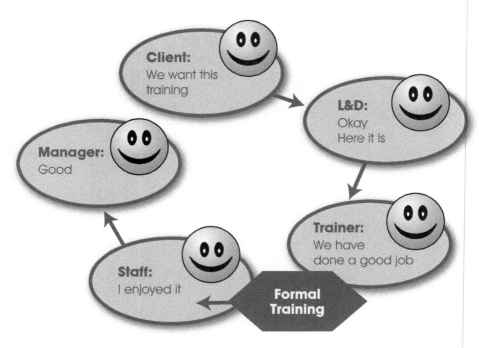

The same "conspiracy" works for I.T. …

> *"We need a new CRM (Customer Relationship Management) system."*

> *"Good – we will build you one."*

… and H.R.

> *"We need to exit these people."*

> *"Okay – this is the process to follow."*

One of the first forms of manipulation we have to cope with is "solutioneering" from line managers, aided by our collusion. I have called this innocent manipulation because it may be just "the way things are done around here" and line managers may not know any differently.

There are other forces that encourage innocent manipulation.

Think about when you are under pressure and you react in a non-rational way.

What do you do?

- "Swear and blame others for your problems."
- "Take it out on someone close to you."
- "Get angry with yourself and snap at other people."
- "Tell a friend how awful 'they' are!"
- "Throw money at the problem."

Fantasy and reality in organisations

Our most common defence reactions are:

- Denial
- Avoidance (hope it goes away)
- Blame someone else
- Moan about it
- Find someone else to give it to
- Ask an expert
- Wait for "the man on the white horse" to solve it for us
- Try a quick fix
- Pay a supplier to take the problem and responsibility away.

Power corrupts; absolute power corrupts absolutely.

The are many truths in this ancient quotation. Psychological experiments have shown significant increases in testosterone when people perceived they had more power than others. In *The Psychologist* (March 2013), Ian Robertson wrote: *"Power may be a cognitive enhancer – even small experimentally induced power levels increase hypocrisy, moral exceptionalism, egocentricity and lack of empathy for others"*.

Abraham Zaleznik (1971) suggests *"Chief executives can also suffer from depersonalisation in their roles and as a result become emotionally cold and detached - paranoid thinking goes beyond suspiciousness, distrust and jealousy. It may take the form of grandiose ideas and overestimation of one's power and control"*.

Fred Goodwin allegedly threatened disciplinary action against staff who allowed cheap pink wafers to be served with the executive coffee. He also insisted all directors wear the company tie and, slightly worse, the RBS recklessly overreached itself by acquiring ABN Amro in 2007. RBS would very likely have survived the 2008 crash if it were not for that decision, which cost £53.5 billion of taxpayers' money!

Take these three forces of:

- "Solutioneering"
- Defence reactions
- The corrupting effect of power

and we end up with the majority of solutions not based on a rational diagnosis of the problem.

In fact, Chris Argyris* thought that over 60% of our current problems are caused by previous solutions!?

> *Chris Argyris*, who died recently, was an American business theorist, Professor Emeritus at Harvard Business School, and a Thought Leader at Monitor Group. He was commonly known for seminal work in the area of "Learning Organizations". (*Wikipedia*)

Another reason why problems may not be faced up to is the **complexity of organisations** and, therefore, of their problems. It is possible that people do not really know where the problems are, how many there are, how they are interlinked and what is causing them.

Defence mechanisms

I believe that most of us use defence mechanisms to protect our fragile self-image and we commonly:

- Project onto others
- Are in denial about problems
- Avoid difficult messages that mean that we have to change.

As Performance Consultants, this **avoidance** and **projection** appears as "**solutioneering**" – the desire to move quickly to solutions that do not involve us in facing up to our own problems and the need to change. I recommend the excellent *Leadership and Self-Deception* (The Arbinger Institute, 1994) which tackles this difficult area of fantasy. The authors use the concept of "**being inside the box**", when we do not "**see**" the reality of our organisations because we are too busy protecting our view of the world with defence mechanisms, hence "inside the box".

To give you an example, I attended a client meeting with a top technical expert who only heard opportunities to display his technical expertise and completely missed the client saying "*So our main concerns are…*" When I repeated this back to him after the meeting he was horrified. He had missed the main point of the meeting by being "inside his own box", and only concerned with how to project his technical competence, in the mistaken belief that was what the client wanted to hear.

Does this mean that the Performance Consulting process cannot work if people are inside their box? Well no, because the process (when used skilfully) actually tackles this whole issue and helps your client to get "out of their box".

The client usually approaches you with an emotional attachment to a brilliant solution ("solutioneering"), so the first stage of the process is all about getting alongside the client, to build enough trust and rapport so that you can work together to reveal the real problem.

The techniques I recommend are:

- go with the flow – repeat back the presenting problem - use the client's words - do not challenge
- match their body language, tone of voice, etc
- turn away from face-to-face towards a "safe" piece of paper
- get the client to draw how they see their world – use a safe open question such as "who is involved in this?"

Once you have built trust and rapport you can start to help the client get out of their box by:

- asking multiple open questions to dig beneath the surface of their defensive generalisations
- comparing where they are now with where they want to get to (the contrast technique)
- introducing anything factual or numeric to help the client face reality and climb out of their box
- picking up on **clues** in their conversation to start to reveal the meaning behind the words and engage at a deeper level. (There will be more on "clues" later.)

What sort of relationship does the client want with you?

Clients say they want internal consultants to:

- Have a thorough grasp of the business
- Appreciate the uniqueness of their situation
- Ask insightful questions
- Possess passion for the task
- Have openness and integrity
- Show flexibility
- Demonstrate willingness to challenge the client.

(ESRC, 2006)

But what do they really think?

In *Managing the Professional Services Firm*, David Maister (2003) explains what it feels like to be a buyer (client). I have modified this to reflect what a business leader might feel about dealing with an H.R./L&D/I.T. internal consultant:

1   I feel **threatened**. *Performance is my accountability, and even though I know I need help, emotionally I am uncomfortable asking for it.*

2   I am **impatient**. *I didn't call someone in at the first sign of the problem symptoms. I have been thinking about this for a while.*

3   I am **worried**. *By the very fact of suggesting improvements, these people are implying that I haven't been doing it right up till now.*

4   I feel **exposed**. *Whoever I talk to I am going to have to reveal my performance.*

5   I feel **ignorant**. *I don't know if I have a simple problem or a complex one. I do not know about the latest thinking on H.R., L&D and I.T.*

6   I am **concerned**. *That they won't take the time to understand what makes my situation special... and will try and push solutions they have, rather than what I need.*

7   I am **suspicious**. *Will they be typical consultants who use jargon and don't explain what they are doing? Consultants always make mountains out of molehills.*

Inspired by David Maister, who finished off by saying:

"In working with an internal consultant I am not just expecting a service I am entering into a relationship. Your selling task is to earn my trust and confidence – with the emphasis on the word 'earn'."

This explains why the first part of the Performance Consulting process is all about building trust and rapport.

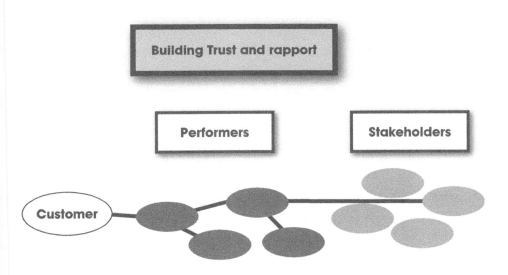

Mapping out who is involved (drawing a rich picture) is actually all about seeing the world as the client sees it and proving that you can listen, be trusted and are worth engaging with.

If you have not built trust and rapport, there is no way that a client will open up to you about their real performance problems.

What is in it for us?

The conspiracy of convenience has existed for years. How are we going to break this group fantasy without suffering push-back and pain? We won't do it unless there is something in it for us.

Someone asked me what I most enjoy about what I do.

I answered that I love solving problems. Reflecting on this:

- I get a buzz from that moment when the client looks you in the eye and says "that's the real problem!"
- I love the feeling of deeper intimacy when you really help people.
- The satisfaction is even greater when you have overcome strong "solutioneering" and avoidance of the real problem.
- Once the real problems are revealed, there is often a release of energy and satisfaction, because we know that we are pursuing solutions that will work.

For the internal consultant, the benefits are:

- An increased credibility with your clients
- Deeper, more honest and rewarding relationships
- A greater sense of self-worth.

For the organisation, we tend to see:

- L&D and H.R. treated as business partners rather than order-takers
- 40% fewer H.R. and L&D solutions
- More measurable business benefits
- A greater variety of H.R. and L&D solutions as part of business solutions.

Summary

There is a whole world of meaning beneath the superficial, about which many people in organisations are unaware. As a result, they end up being manipulated and pushed around by others who have power and influence over their lives.

In most cases, this is innocent collusion and many people in junior positions do not realise the tactics and manipulation used by people "above" them.

As an internal consultant (H.R., L&D or I.T.) you need to be aware of the irrational part of the organisation, because it may be trying to manipulate you into providing easy solutions which, whilst appearing to be very positive, can actually be just expensive ways of avoiding the real business problems.

Part of your responsibility is to:

- Make sure that investment in your solutions are linked to business value.
- Ensure that you are skilled enough to engage with your clients at a level of intimacy and credibility so that you tackle the real issues and are not just an "order-taker" for "solutioneering" and quick fixes.

The benefits of "solutioneering" are enormous. You need to be aware of this and know how to deal with it if you are going to be successful as an internal consultant.

To make things easy, we are going to group manipulative tactics together, and first we will see how to deal with innocent manipulation.

Time for reflection

Think about your experience of power and solutioneering.

Can you recognise cases when:

I   The solution did not solve the "real" problem.
2   Someone "pushed" through a solution using their power.
3   You felt "steam rollered" into a decision.
4   An interaction with your client just felt "off" or wrong and you don't know why?

Innocent manipulation?

Dealing with Innocent Manipulation

What is it?

My experience is that most people are honest and will work in a rational way to solve performance problems, as long as you start your consulting in a positive, authentic and trusting way.

Innocent manipulation happens when the people you are dealing with are good people within a dysfunctional system. A line manager may believe that training is **the solution** to their problem and that your role is to be an "**order taker**" to deliver that solution. As an "order taker" you just need to be told enough:

> *"We need you to organise this training."*

This sort of innocent manipulation is relatively easy to deal with:

1   You **can** choose to behave in a superficial way and **accept the order,** in which case when the training does not deliver the desired performance you can claim innocence: "*I was just doing my job, people liked the training, here are the happy sheets to prove it.*" This is one way of behaving.

2   You can choose to be more professional and ask some questions, to make sure the solutions will meet your clients requirements:

> *"Who do you want this for?"*
> *"What are they doing now?"*
> *"What do you want them to be able to do?"*
> *"What would be the cost of doing nothing?"*
> *"If the solution is successful, what would you see happening?"*

(Otherwise known as the 7-step Performance Consulting process).

To remind you, this process covers:

The Performance Consulting Process

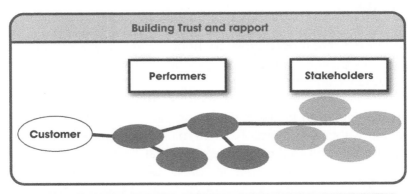

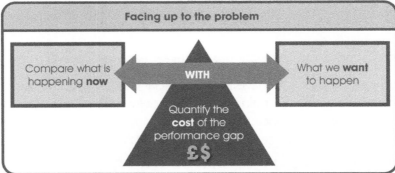

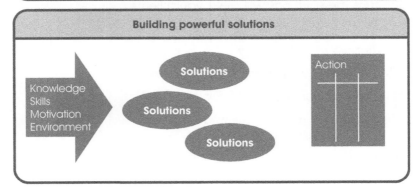

Most clients will react positively to this professional approach and will "let you in" on the real business issues behind the superficial request for an instant solution like "*they need training*". The performance consulting process works very well here and you usually:

- Stop "solutioneering"
- Identify the real performance problems
- Design joint solutions that will work
- Build your credibility, respect and influence with your customers
- Move towards being a True Business Partner.

I think the biggest reason for innocent manipulation is the pay off for jumping to quick solutions ("solutioneering").

Spotting innocent manipulation

The "Everything Goes Well" story

You are Ted, the Learning and Development Manager, and your client Jane contacts you about a "Training Need":

"Ted, we need more sales training by June."

You have a good relationship with Jane and you ask her some questions.

Ted: "Okay, so you need sales training by June. How long have you got to discuss it now?"

Jane: "Fifteen minutes."

Ted: "May I ask you some questions, so that I can get to the bottom of your requirements and put together a business case?"

Jane: "Okay."

Ted: "Who do you want the sales training for?"

Jane: "The sales team."

Ted: "Is that UK or Sweden?"

Jane: "UK."

Ted: "So what is happening now?"

Jane: "We need to train the UK guys."

Ted: "Okay ... Imagine we had trained them, what would we see happening?"

Jane: "They wouldn't be lagging behind in adopting the new way of selling."

Ted: "And how much is this lag?"

Jane: "The Swedes started working in bid teams and have made two corporate sales."

Ted: "Oh, how much is that worth?"

Jane: "A million dollars each."

Ted: "And what about the UK?"

Jane: "They say they will form the new teams, but they are so busy hitting their personal targets that I know they have missed two opportunities for a global deal because our competitor won them."

Ted: "So, if we don't do anything about this, what would the cost be?"

Jane: "About five million in lost sales if we do not get our act together."

Ted: "Wow! Let's have a look at some of the reasons for this gap. I guess the UK guys are the main players?"

Jane: "Yes."

Ted: "Firstly, do they know how to sell?"

Jane: "Yes, they all completed the sales training last year."

Ted: "Oh, so they have had training?"

Jane: "Yes!"

Ted: "Do they know how to sell in bid teams?"

Jane: "No, they are resisting setting them up."

Ted: "Are they motivated to work in bid teams?"

Jane: "No, they still have to meet their individual targets and the only way they can do this is to sell what, and how, they already know."

Ted: "Is that the main reason for the performance gap?"

Jane: "Yes, you are right. Thank goodness I talked to you first before booking the training! Thanks Ted, you are a mate, and I will talk to you earlier next time."

In an ideal world, our conversations might go like that, but often the client is avoiding facing up to their problems by asking for a quick fix.

The "Innocent Manipulation" version

You are Ted, the Learning and Development Manager, and your client Jean contacts you about a "Training Need":

"Ted, we need more sales training by June."

You have a good relationship with Jean and you ask her some questions.

Ted: "Okay, so you need sales training by June. How long have you got to discuss it now?"

Jean: "Fifteen minutes."

Ted: "May I ask you some questions so that I can get a good picture of your requirements and put together a business case?"

Jean: "Okay, but we need to get something by June because the European Sales Conference is in London on June 5th and I want to do something by then!"

Ted: "Who do you want the sales training for?"

Jean: "The sales team."

Ted: "Is that just UK, or Sweden as well?"

Jean: "Both, they all need it – that is, all the managers should do it together. I have set aside two days – is your sales trainer guy available? I hope so – can you ring him now?"

Ted: "I will check as soon as I have asked you a few questions. So what is happening now?"

Jean: "We need to train the UK guys."

Ted: "Okay ... Imagine we had trained them. What would we see happening?"

Jean: "They wouldn't be lagging behind in adopting the new way of selling."

Ted: "Ah ha! And how much is this lag?"

Jean: "Look, I just need to make sure that they have all been trained okay. The Board have agreed to the budget, we just need to get everyone on board and working the same way – consistent selling, that is what I want."

Ted: "So if we don't do anything about this, what would the cost be?"

Jean: "We will miss an opportunity when all the sales managers are together and we still have time to influence the annual sales figures. Can you see why this is so urgent? Sorry, I have to go now. Thanks for getting this organised, Ted. If your guy is not available I know someone we could use."

Jean is using innocent manipulation. She is under pressure and thinking inside her own box. In this case, she is manipulating you, but it is innocent manipulation or "solutioneering".

The enormous benefits of "solutioneering"

Forces which encourage innocent "solutioneering":

- Pressure to come up with solutions rather than problems.
- It just the way things are done around here.
- How the L&D function has positioned itself as the organiser of instant solutions, e.g. "sales training".

- Line managers feel it is their job to analyse business problems and do not see why they need to share this with the training supplier.
- We all talk in generalisations rather than detail – "We need sales training" is merely a handy way to discuss a complex topic.
- We all jump to conclusions too quickly and find comfort in framing problems as solutions.

- The human desire to make sense of complexity, to turn the fluid into concrete, randomness into patterns (See Gestalt Theory).
- In order to protect our self-image, we project onto others, and avoid the effort of difficult changes that we have to make.

How to manage innocent manipulation

So how do we deal with this "steamrollering"?

- Do **not** challenge the fantasy, but work with the energy of the "quick-fix solutioneering" by working with urgency.
- **Recognise** (by repeating the client's words) the suggested solution, but do not accept responsibility.

- **Ask open questions** to get the client to open up around the real performance problem without challenging them: "**Who** needs this training?", "**What** is happening now?"
- Encourage the client to **work with us to map out** where they see the problem: "Who is involved?"

- **Build trust** by active listening and authenticity.
- Listen for **key words** and clues so that we can reveal a deeper level of meaning, intimacy and challenge.
- Build enough **rapport** so that we can help the client face up to the real problem: "What is happening now?", "What do you want to happen?"
- **Quantify** what this (the performance gap) means to the client: "What will this cost if we do nothing?"
- Use a rational/diagnostic approach to **investigate causes** for the performance gap, and link together a range of solutions including management action.
- **Build an adult-adult relationship** with the client, so they respect your partnership in working with them to improve the performance and results of their team. See example on following page.

Repeat back the client's words to prove that you are listening to them	"You need xx training"
Ask for permission to ask questions	"Is it okay if I ask you some questions?"
Start by opening up the problem around the system that performs	"Who do you want this for?" "Is anyone else involved?"
Expose the current performance	"What are they doing now?"
Visualise the desired state	"What do we want them to be able to do?"
Quantify the cost of the gap	"What would be the cost of doing nothing about this?"
Let's identify some possible solutions	"How could we provide better **knowledge**?" "How can they improve their **skills**?" "How can we improve the **motivation** to achieve the desired performance?" "Are there any **other obstacles** that we can remove?"
Agree an action plan	"What shall we try first?"

As internal consultants, we have to be very careful to build the right level of trust and awareness to help clients face up to their own problems.

Part of building this trust with the client is to start to see the world from their point of view. This is why we draw a simple system diagram of the people involved, which usually ends up as a shared "map" of where the problems are.

Imagine you are talking to a friend who asks if you would recommend golf clubs because they are thinking of buying some new ones. You might assume that this is a simple problem with a single person involved.

But even this apparently simple problem actually involves a system, e.g.

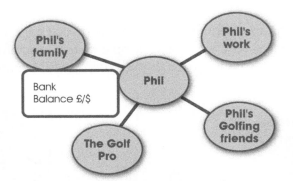

You would be behaving irresponsibly if you recommended a particular set of clubs without knowing more about him, his goals, how much he can afford, etc.

Buying new golf clubs is just about the simplest performance problem I can think of. All work issues are much more complex.

Here is an example of a typical system diagram at work:

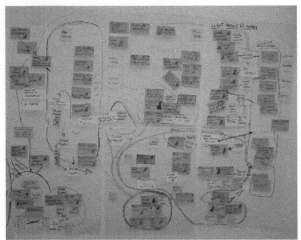

In my experience, most organisations are irrational/emotional places, where "solutioneering" is rife. On my skills workshops I always ask the same question and always find that my clients estimate that more than 60% of their current problems are caused by previous solutions. L&D teams often suffer from a lack of power and credibility, along with unrealistic expectations for training, which is seen as an act of faith rather than something that has a measurable value to the business.

To build the credibility and effectiveness of internal consultants we need to engage as business partners and help our clients to face up to the real performance problems that exist behind their attempts to jump to quick solutions.

Innocent manipulation does not only happen at work

It happened to me last night.

My wife asked me to take our freezer up to church (an instant solution) because she is running a café at the church fete this Saturday and had ordered some ice cream to sell.

Her instant solution was that I would solve the problem for her by taking our freezer to the church (I would take the problem away from her). I thought this was a bad idea but instead of pushing back I asked about **who is involved**:

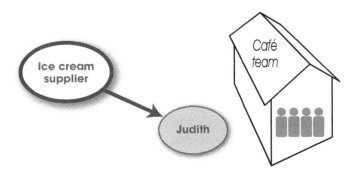

The ice cream supplier – Judith and the café team – the church – the church fete

How are things now?

- Ice cream to be collected the day before the fete
- Café set up in the church
- No way to store the ice cream

What does she want?

- To be able to sell the ice cream

Possible solutions

1. Our freezer: will not fit in our car – difficult to transport – full of our stuff.
2. Use cool boxes with ice: much more portable than our domestic freezer.

Judith decided on using the cool boxes and freezing more ice in our freezer.

She felt relieved about the solution. (I think she knew that the freezer solution was a classic case of "solutioneering" and she was setting me up but just could not think of anything else when under pressure.)

Group think

Another reason why we take such poor decisions and tend to jump to easy solutions is the pressure for conformity in groups. It is very hard to analyse the complex cause behind organisational problems when you are under the pressure of working in a group (say 3–4 people). Add more people and the results can be disastrous. Anyone brave enough to make a proposal will either be shouted down, or supported with little analysis of the problem. The classic case in history is President Kennedy and the Bay of Pigs fiasco, when Kennedy made a terrible decision that no one really agreed with. Less well known are the many group compromises in church halls and golf clubs, where a large committee agrees to something that no one really believes in, but dares not challenge.

Every organisational problem occurs within a complex system and in reality will always need multiple solutions to be successful. Single solutions never work.

I think that many problem-solving sessions, with their formal agendas, board room tables, PowerPoint presentations and linear thinking, cannot cope with the complexity of the problems they are trying to solve.

Someone once said:

> *"For every problem there is a simple cost-effective solution and it is always wrong."*

But, in the hurly-burly of a painful board meeting, this sort of "silver bullet" proposal is just the one that gets voted into agreement.

For example, a top UK supermarket agreed to commission "creativity training sessions" for their managers. None of the directors challenged this simplistic solution and the Training Director was commissioned to organise the solution. The workshops were fun and well-received but six months later the company still fell further behind its main rival due to the dullness of its product range. The solution had been well organised by the Training Department but it was never going to solve the real business problem because the real business problem had not been exposed.

Group problem analysis

Keeping in mind the idea that people need to feel that it was their decision, one good way to win over stakeholders is to invite them to a problem analysis session, where you take the stakeholders through the process to analyse the problem from their perspective, and then agree action.

Dealing with Innocent Manipulation

This works very well if you can get all the stakeholders in a room together to work through the performance consulting process. The practical things to remember are:

- Allow enough space – book a big room with a blank wall.
- Allow plenty of time – 2 to 3 hours for 3 to 4 people.
- Remove the tables and place the chairs in a semi-circle facing the blank wall.
- Stick flip charts on the wall showing the 7-step process headings.
- At the start, make sure you encourage rapport between people with an introductions exercise.
- You may fill in some of the flip charts with your current thinking but leave the solutions and action plan blank so that the team can make their own decisions.

By the end of the session, all the stakeholders should buy in to the agreed action plan.

I run such strategic sessions for boards of directors.

- In one example, the board wanted to start a new company even though the current business was not performing and setting up the new venture would take energy and resources away from the real problems. When we drew the diagram this became obvious and they re-focused on overcoming the threats to the current business.
- In another example, a government body wanted to outsource their recruitment at a cost of £6 million. When we drew the diagram it revealed that internal recruitment processes only took six weeks of the six month delay and the problem lay elsewhere in the diagram. Spending £6 million on outsourcing would not have solved the problem.
- An underperforming European sales team wanted to develop a new sales strategy to enter new markets. When we drew the system diagram it was obvious that the quickest way to improve sales was from existing clients and contracts, which held 25 times as much potential value as the risky new venture.

In all cases I help my clients to face up to their issues using a system diagram (usually on 6–8 flip charts on a wall). The next step is always to prioritise their goals and allocate clear accountability.

As Performance Consultants we often have to help our clients to face up to their responsibilities.

Summary

In order to cope with innocent manipulation, use the Performance Consulting process and your consulting skills to work with your client in partnership, to help them face their real problems.

But what do you do when your clients continue to resist your honest efforts to work with them?

2

What is it?

Some of your clients will resist your professional approach. They might go along with "who do you want the training for?" but they will try and keep the interaction with you **on a superficial level**:

"Everyone needs the training, when can you deliver?"

If you try and probe further:

"Can I ask you some questions to make sure I am clear about your requirements?"

You may get straight resistance:

"No, we have agreed they need more sales training" (You are not important enough to have been involved) *"I have the budget"* (I am more powerful than you) *"When can you arrange a two-day course for all my sales teams?"* (I want you to take my order).

(You have been told what the method is and it is clear they expect you to act as a non-questioning **"order taker"**.)

In this case the client is resisting interaction with you on an equal level and is using power to resist facing up to the real problems. It is a classic negotiating position, and you also need to adopt a negotiating approach rather than rational joint problem-solving.

Basically, you counter the uses of power with power. More later.

I think the biggest reason behind powerful resistance is that your client has made a hasty commitment to a quick solution with powerful stakeholders and then does not want to lose face.

It is only when you lose trust and rapport and the client continues to resist a rational approach to analyse the real problem that we switch our tactics.

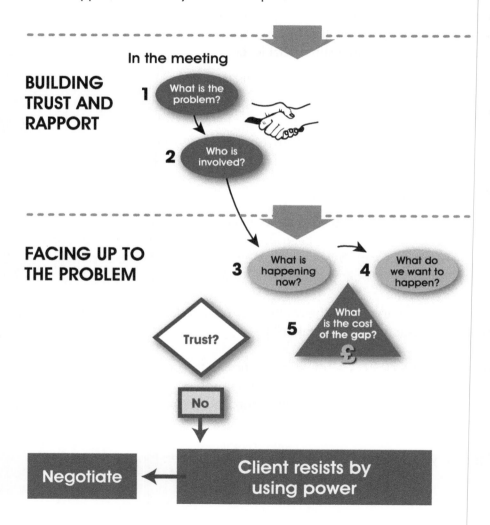

Spotting powerful resistance

A story

You are Ted, the Learning and Development Manager, and your client John contacts you about a "Training Need":

Ted, we need more sales training by June.

> *"Good to see you, Ted. Listen, I have to catch a plane. Just wanted to let you know that we discussed sales training at the executive last night. Well, it was on the golf course actually. I got them to agree to a £650,000 budget for a completely new sales training initiative to help us achieve our strategic objectives. I have mentioned it to Jim at BetterSales Inc. You know him, don't you? Good supplier. Please can you get it organised. Oh, I said we would get something started by June - okay? Got to rush - good to see you. How is your golf?"*

John is dropping so many hints about how powerful he is and how he just expects you to be a "pair of hands". In this case, joint problem-solving will not work. You need to decide whether to confront his power or just go ahead with the current unwritten contract.

You inner dialogue will be something like:

- Is it worth challenging him?
- How much power does he have?
- How much do I have?
- Is it worth it?

If you decide that it **is** worth challenging him, then you are into a negotiation.

In *How to be A True Business Partner (Harrison, 2008)* we covered:

Power play – negotiation

Client Resists by Using Power

The simplest use of power is the power to say *"Just do what I say!"* This can be a very straightforward *"Just do it!"*, or it can be after a period of pretend listening, after which the client states their ideas again.

Client	Our response
"Just do it!"	*"It may not be the best solution."*
I want to create the appearance of action —"Just do it!"	*This quick fix will not work —"What is the problem we are trying to solve?"*
It is not an important project for me, it does not warrant my attention —"Just do it!"	*"?!"*

The key thing to recognise in situations like this is that **you are not in joint problem-solving mode, so rational argument will not work!**

The only things that work with a power player are either using opposing power or compliance. You are in a **bargaining** meeting, where the decision over action will depend on who has the most power, **NOT** on what is the best thing for the organisation.

If you decide to use your power, then you could be into a bargaining negotiation, where the first person makes a high bid and the opponent starts as low as they dare.

Client	Our response
"Just do it!"	*"No – It may not be the best solution."*
"I want it done!"	*"We cannot justify spending £100k on a quick fix that might not work."*
"But I need action by June."	*"What do you need to see by June?"*
"Some training courses completed."	*"Why?"*
"It is the sales conference and I promised the Board that I would arrange some more sales training."	*"Let me quickly look at the problem and we will produce some evidence of sales training interventions by June, but I need your help in looking at the real problem."*
"No, just organise the training."	*"What do you want the training to achieve?"*
"More sales: leave it to me to just organise more sales training for everyone by June."	*"No, we cannot justify a quick fix for £100k."*
"But it's my budget – just do it."	*"I may be able to do that if you give me a week to complete the needs analysis. Otherwise, I cannot support using £100k on sales training."*

Some bargaining principles

In classic bargaining, people start high and progressively move to a compromise.

Two men haggling over a car

The buyer wants to spend £3,900; the seller wants to sell for £4,100.

Buyer	Seller
"How much?" *(Never move first.)*	"£4,500."
"Oh!... Now, it's not worth that much." *(Try to make him move down first.)*	"Well, I would accept £4,400."*(Only move in small steps.)*
"It is 5 years old and the price guide says £3,700 is a good price." *(Low opening bid uses first bit of information.)*	"But this is in excellent condition. In my guide the top guide price is more like £4,200, and this also has a low mileage." *(Plays his first bit of information.)* "How much can you afford?"
"I can afford plenty but I want a fair price – how about £3,800?"	"Well, I want £4,200 and you are offering £3,800 – how about if we split the difference and agree on £4,000? After all, it is fully taxed." *(Plays final bargaining chip.)*

In bargaining, people tend to move to a compromise

And remember to only share information one piece at a time.

The trick is to recognise when you are in a bargaining meeting. If you are, the tricks of game are:

- Work out your power versus their power.
- Get them to start first.
- Only give away a little at a time.
- If you have to give something away, make sure that you win a concession from them.
- Have a final bargaining chip ready (to throw in to close the deal).

If you are having "problems" with a "difficult" client, you need to decide:

- Have you really understood their view of the world?
- Have you built sufficient rapport and trust?
- Is joint problem-solving working?
- Are they using power, are you in a bargaining meeting?

And then:

- If you are in a bargaining meeting, what power do you have?
- Switch to a bargaining strategy.

Calculate your power versus their power and their likely bargaining ploys.

In the case of John, we decide to stand up to his use of power by using some of our own.

> *"Sorry John, I cannot agree to an investment of company money until we have done the business case, so we need about 30 minutes so I can ask you a few questions. When can we meet, to do this? If you need something by June, we had better get started."*

Realistically how much power do we have?

As an H.R., L&D or I.T. consultant, in most organisations your sources of power are likely to be:

- Your personal credibility and track record.
- Your consulting skills, used to analyse the real causes of the problem and present a superbly logical set of winning solutions that are better than the quick fix.
- The ability to say NO to investment in solutions within your expertise, e.g. Training, H.R. and I.T.
- Control over budget.
- Your ability to slow such projects down.

Let's use the sources of power as an additional checklist:

PHYSICAL POWER	Intimidate them by being bigger, stronger, more beautiful
RESOURCE	Control reward Can you hold back evidence that they need for their performance reviews?
POSITION	Involve your boss
CONTROL	Restrict access to stakeholders within your influence
EXPERT	Stress your information and expertise about solutions to similar cases that resulted in increased business
CHARISMA	Be confident, look them in the eye, keep still, adopt a posture of relaxed power
LEGITIMATE	Stress that you have a consensus from the Executive to ask questions about the performance problem before you are allowed to agree to expensive solutions
NEGATIVE	Hold back information Delay or do not complete agreed actions
OVERT	Stress that you have to follow the agreed process – show them the forms
COVERT	Explain that performance consulting is "The way things work around here"
PERSONAL	Demonstrate your ability to ask open question, listen, build trust and rapport Display your expertise and competence in valued solutions Be charming, charismatic, attractive, and fun to work with Be authentic at all times and build trust and loyalty

Aim for partnership

INTERNALISED	The client leaves the meeting thinking the action plan was their own idea

Summary

If you are in a meeting and you lose trust, and the client resorts to telling you to do the solution…

Try to level with the client and re-establish rapport. Then continue with trust and use the Performance Consulting process and your consulting skills to avoid "solutioneering" and help the client to face up to the real business problem.

AND IF THIS DOES NOT WORK …

Recognise that you are in a negotiation – work out your power and *negotiate.*

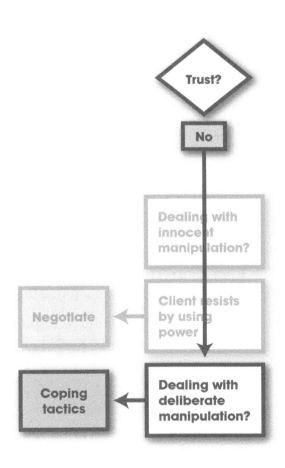

What is deliberate manipulation?

Some people have got to positions of power through their skills in manipulation, impression management and cunning. It is said that 3% of the population have psychopathic tendencies. These are:

- Charm
- Lack of conscience
- Drive for dominance
- Love of physical possession.

Organisations tend to reward such behaviour. The problem with dealing with manipulators is that, if we hold on to our view of the world as a rational and fair place, then we often fail to understand or recognise people who are not playing by our rules.

For example, we may think that a senior manager would not:

- Overtly lie
- Do something that will damage the customer
- Do things that are not to the benefit of the organisation.

But these are our unhelpful assumptions. In many organisations, there are people commissioning projects that will have no benefit to the customer or the organisation, but may:

- Make them look good in the short-term
- Give the impression of energy, action and success
- Leave other people looking bad.

In order to cope with really manipulative people, I suggest we need to be aware of them and their tactics and try to keep out of their way as much as possible.

I think the biggest reason for deliberate manipulation is raw pursuit of power and lack of empathy for anyone else's needs.

How to spot deliberate manipulation

A story

You are Ted, the Learning and Development Manager, and James contacts you about a "Training Need":

Ted, we need more sales training by June

> *"Good to see you, Ted. I hear great things about you. Listen, we have a very important project - not many people could handle this but I think you can."*
>
> *"Just wanted to let you know that we discussed sales training at the Executive last night. I have managed to get you a £650,000 budget for a completely new sales training initiative."*
>
> *"I thought you would be pleased. Only you need to deliver quickly so I have arranged for you to meet Jim at BetterSales Inc. You know him, don't you? In this case we can ignore the rule on getting three quotes."*
>
> *"Keep me informed. How about a game of golf with me and Jim on Saturday? You can brief me on progress then."*

James is bending the company rules here and involving in you in the conspiracy.

A straight negotiation will not work.

You inner dialogue will be something like:

- I need to avoid this trap
- How do I get out of here and find support?
- What tactics can I use now to escape to fight another day?

Don't commit yourself to anything.

James is playing a psychological game with you.

- Do something unexpected (to break the pattern)
- Make no commitment
- Just get out of there!

For example, "Oh, sorry James, I have forgotten the time! I need to be somewhere else, now – got to go!... Talk to you later..."

Then go and discuss James's attempted manipulation with your boss and get them involved in the next stage.

What happens when you do not trust your client?

The majority of your performance consulting meetings will be successful if you use a rational, joint problem-solving approach, and even powerful, manipulative people will change their behaviour if you are open and honest. If you are in a supportive meeting, these people are usually carried along with the group ethos and will not expose themselves. However, there will be times when people are playing games.

You might notice this from your feelings at the time:

- Things don't feel quite right
- You don't really trust what someone is saying
- One person is speaking too much and with too much intensity.

Trust your feelings – you are probably right, there may well be something going on below the apparent interactions. The secret is to be sensitive to your feelings, and then use this awareness to choose how to react in a flexible way.

What is game playing?

Eric Berne's *Games People Play* (1964), is a very accessible book describing our personality and ego states in terms of:

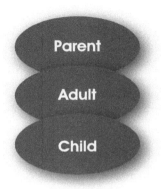

(See *How to be a True Business Partner*.) Clients might use a powerful position to get you to promise more than you ought to:

> *"I am sure that we will have no problems now that you are our business partner, Ted."*

> *"I just need you to commit to all the sales force being trained by April."*

Watch out for praise and sweeping solutions that **you** have to deliver! They may be setting you up in a game called NIGYSOB ("Now I have Got You, You Son Of a Bitch").

The following is an extract from *How to be a True Business Partner* by *Performance Consulting* (Harrison, 2008). Berne called his theory Transactional Analysis, partly because he saw effective communication between people as straightforward transactions. For example, when you are in a child state (having fun) and relate to others in a child state, this is an appropriate transaction.

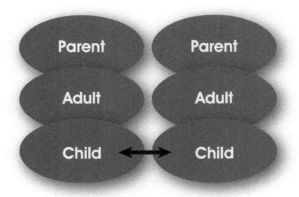

However, Berne saw that interactions could also be crossed, e.g. a "parent" message from someone:

"Keep your shoes shiny, young man"

... could **hook** a "child" reaction of:

"Push off, Grandad!"

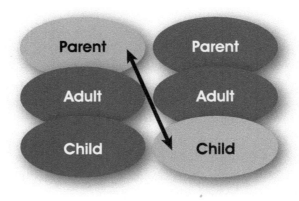

The "ideal" state for effective communication at work is adult – adult. Berne also explains how many transactions are deliberately crossed and manipulative. He calls these psychological games.

NIGYSOB – Now I have Got You, You Son Of a Bitch

This is when someone praises you and sets you up to take full responsibility for a task:

"Yes Chris, we selected you for this important project because you are excellent at handling these special difficulties."

NIGYSOB is often associated with expecting you to be a "pair of hands" consultant or order-taker:

"We need the solution ready by April for the launch of the new product. Your predecessor could not have met such tight deadlines but we are sure that, with your ability, you can manage it."

I was in a client executive meeting last week when the Chief Executive turned to the L&D Consultant and said: *"But we will be okay now because we have training on board and we are going to train them all."* He smiled as he said it and the other board members shared his game. They did not believe that training was the solution but were used to trying it on with the Training Manager. This one responded defensively, assertively and stood her ground, saying that training was not the whole solution and she would not be set up for a fall.

Can you think of any times when you have been set up in this way? Game playing is deliberate manipulation.

Some of the consultants that I train complain about feeling "steamrollered". Their clients often refer to a person with power as "X says", giving the impression that the solution has already been decided and cannot be questioned. They are passing you a non-negotiable order, e.g. "X (our common boss) says we need this, when can you deliver?" or "The board wants to see this by April – I am sure that you can deliver." Both of these are examples of reference to higher power and treating you as an "order taker".

How to manage game playing and manipulation

Some managers are so attached to their powerful positions that they find it very difficult to accept any challenge from you, a lower status supplier, and they react in a parental way, preventing you from understanding the real performance problem.

They may have their own reasons for wanting a quick fix, and will move the spotlight from them to you, wanting to avoid any exposure of the current performance gap with their team!

My advice is that it is hard to change another person's behaviour but you can change your own.

Start all new relationships on a rational, authentic basis and the client will usually react in a similar way, e.g.

Clarify your role

*"My role is to work with you to make sure we can deliver solutions that meet **your** requirements."*

Explain the process you will use

"In order to make sure that we meet your requirement, we have a process to make sure that we are crystal clear about it before we commission any solutions."

"My job is to work with you to check your requirements. I will bring in other specialists as necessary."

Finally, move to physical rapport by asking

"Can we start to map out who will use this CRM package?"

At the same time, produce a blank sheet of paper and intimate that this is where you want to record the information. Push it across the desk or ask:

"Can we sit here so we can draw it together?"

Be authentic – explain why you are doing this:

"So that I have a good idea of who needs this solution."

These stages can be used to move someone away from "solutioneering" – you can move to sitting side-by-side which encourages joint problem-solving.

Remember to keep using "we" and match their body language and tone of voice.

In most cases the client will be happy to investigate the problem and work rationally.

If the client responds negatively, you now have a different interaction to manage and you will have to alter your behaviour to be more defensive:

- **If they are playing games you need to try to get them back to adult – adult.**
- If they are playing power, you may have to respond with power and treat the meeting as a negotiation (and you need to be ready to quit the meeting).
- Sometimes you might agree to give the client what they want (if it does not cost too much and will not do harm).
- Sometimes you will just have to accept that the client is not ready for a joint problem-solving relationship.

In all cases you need to handle the emotional relationship before moving on to the task.

There is no magic answer for how to deal with game playing, the use and abuse of power or manipulation.

Some tips:

- Trust your feelings – if something feels "a bit off", it probably is.
- Don't react emotionally.
- Stop the conversation if you recognise that you are getting angry or disturbed and cannot work out why.
- Listen to your thoughts – if "this sounds too good to be true" then it probably is!
- React in an adult way.
- Ask questions.
- Keep things rational – stick to facts.
- Read up about psychological games so that you can spot them.
- If you are in a game, do something different.
- Get out of the interaction – make some excuse and give yourself time to reflect on what has been going on. Discuss it with a friend.

If you find that you are reacting as either angry child or angry parent, then you are giving away much of your power in the relationship and you are being manipulated by the other person.

Let's get inside the head of a manipulative person

Imagine that I am your worst nightmare of a boss. The first thing that you need to realise about me is that I do not care about you. In fact, my locus of control (the extent to which individuals believe that they can control events that affect them) is almost totally internal. I do not seek or recognise the feelings or good opinion of my colleagues or subordinates. The only people whose opinions I care about are those with power or influence over me and my future prospects.

I do not socialise outside work. I found it hard to build lasting relationships at school. I am married to a similar person. Our house is immaculate. We have the latest car and gadgets, and no children. We both take extreme care over our appearance.

The thing that really bothers me is results. I will pore over spreadsheets for hours to make sure that all my figures are defendable. I always do this before I go at any internal meeting where I might be assessed. I work long hours and am totally focused on achieving the next promotion. No one can criticise my effort or results.

The other strange thing about me is that I have few feelings of guilt and I have virtually no conscience. I am smart and charming and see every interaction as a game that I need to win. I am totally competitive, shallow and driven by achievement, expensive objects and success.

This is what I think of my colleagues ...

Learning and Development

They are useful, naïve and helpful people. My aim is to get hold of as much of the training budget for my department as I can. I want to give the impression to senior managers that I develop my people and that lots of interesting training initiatives are happening in my patch.

When I spot a problem like low sales or low individual performance, I always involve training. This is for four reasons:

- Training is a free resource which might solve the problem for me.
- If they fail, I can always blame them.
- They are nice, enthusiastic people who will not challenge me.
- My staff like the attention and will thank me for the development opportunity.

This is how it goes:

"Hi L&D person, please come to my office to discuss our L&D requirements."

"Good to see you, sorry but I only have 20 minutes before the regional executive meeting. We have discussed our goals for the rest of the year and want to provide sales coaching for all the team leaders. Please could you arrange that? We have a special problem with Veronica – I think she needs some assertiveness training, can you research into that?"

I.T.

I think I.T. people are slightly different to the L&D team. The I.T. people are all nerdy, introverted, and love new stuff and jargon. I handle them slightly differently.

This is how it goes:

"Hi I.T., have you heard about integrated, handheld CRM technology? Our competitors are using it. I want to see if we can get handhelds and instant quotes for my sales people. No one else has done it here before. Do you think we can look into it? I have a bit of budget – can you buy one so we can test the concept? We might need to alter our system slightly but I think you could do it."

H.R.

H.R. is a harder nut to manipulate. They tend to be more savvy and hold informational power; they like to be expert consultants but they have little business acumen or experience.

This is how it goes:

> *"Hello H.R., please can we have a meeting to discuss how we exit a problem employee? I am just about to give him a written warning and want to check with you that we are following the right procedure. I know we have to be watertight on these cases."*

Waiters and support staff

If I calculate that people have much less power than me then I treat them with disdain. I ignore waiters, snap out my orders and never leave a tip. They are not worth my time. However, if people could be useful to me (like the chairman's chauffeur), I ingratiate myself with superficial banter.

This is how I influence people

As an experienced manipulator, I have flexed my style and language to match the people I want to influence:

- I perceive the L&D person as the least powerful and, with their preference for being helpful, I act as an enthusiastic order giver.
- I talk to the I.T. person with lots of jargon about solutions and give them a juicy problem to solve.
- I am more wary of H.R. and appeal to their status as experts and protectors of correct process.
- I just tell waiters what I want.

Reading people more powerful than me

I pride myself on my ability to "read" people.

Dealing with Real Manipulation

I will take a bit of time to find out about important people before I meet them. I keep up with the gossip, have a look at their LinkedIn and Facebook pages, and talk to colleagues about what sort of person they are.

I am looking for:

- Whether they are "moving away" or a "moving towards" person
- A feeling or factual person
- A big picture or sequential person.

When I meet you, I keep still and look in to your eyes. Do you respond or look away? I feel for your power in your handshake. Do you have natural, relaxed Chi or are you tense and weak?

I trust my natural instinct about how powerful you are compared with me.

Then I listen for clues in your language. Phrases such as:

- "Opportunity to"
- "I feel we would really benefit from"
- "It would be a great thing for everyone"

make me read you as:

- "Opportunity to"   moving towards person
- "I feel"   feeling person
- "Great for everyone"   big picture person

So, I change my language to be comfortable for you:

Positive words about what we could do, moving towards a big picture of the benefits…

In this way I "read" you and flex my behaviour to fit in with what you want to hear.

Levels of intimacy

The first level of intimacy

I have a starting position with each supplier. I am trying to get them to achieve what I want with minimum challenge and involvement from me. A successful meeting is when the supplier "takes" the bait and offers to help with a solution that they will own and do most of the work towards.

This is what I call an easy meeting

I try and engage with everyone at work in a superficial way. "Hi, how are you?" Then move straight on to "How are the figures looking? What can we do to reach this period's targets?" I do the same with internal suppliers but occasionally I come up against a more skilful opponent.

If I have to socialise with colleagues, I stick to safe topics like football, cars, sport and jokes, and I converse in a superficial way. I speak in generalisations such as "they always miss penalties" and "referees are getting worse these days". I can keep this level of non-intimacy up for years, especially with male "friends".

The second level of intimacy

I always start with the same opening gambit, which requires no disclosure from me and is tempting bait for the supplier to "take" the order. Occasionally someone (a self-aware L&D person for example) will not take the initial "bait" but will look me in the eye and ask me some questions. In this case, I know that they are challenging me to engage on a deeper level. If an L&D person gets me to open up about who I want the solution for I can hardly refuse, and I often answer this question but stay as vague as possible to see if they are prepared to push further.

However, if an L&D person really listens and gets me talking about the problem, they can encourage me to open up more than I was expecting to. If they do this with skill and confidence I might let them in and open up to a second level of intimacy. This is very rare.

I find that H.R. people tend to have more self-awareness and skill in dealing with people like me. Once they fail to take the bait, they like to assert their power, and as long as I "ask" for their expert opinion, they are fine. We often continue as equals. I will tell them as little as I need to about a particular individual and they will help me to get rid of them with the correct process.

If I perceive that an internal supplier has:

- Personal credibility and power
- Skilful conversational control and listening
- Positional power
- Information power
- Control over budget

then I might engage with them at the second level of intimacy, where I am prepared to share information about the business problem in return for something.

The third level of intimacy

This supplier really understands me. I can see how, if I work with them and share what I really want, I can get there even quicker than if I keep information close to my chest. I respect them, they see the world the way I do and are a pleasure to do business with. I might invite them for a competitive game of squash. It would be fun. I respect them and their skills.

These levels of intimacy do not really exist, but the principle is that people will engage with you on different levels. Most open, honest people can move quickly from superficial to intimate, as long as the signals they receive are positive and authentic. Some naïve and less aware people are deceived by the easy rapport of the slick salesperson. They think "*he is a nice guy*", but they do not recognise that they are being worked or manipulated.

So you think it couldn't happen?

One of my friends described the behaviour of their boss whom I suggested might be a psychopath.

The lack of conscience and immense charm had made her very successful in the short term, but she left a trail of ruined personal and private relationships behind her.

At my suggestion my client read *Snakes in Suits* (Babiak and Hare, 2006) and agreed with my diagnosis.

We thought his options were:

- Avoid her as much as possible
- Don't listen to a thing she says, just watch what she does
- Look for another job.

In reality he did all of these. If you are within the net of a powerful and manipulative person, probably the best thing you can do is to remove yourself from the situation – you are unlikely to change their behaviour.

Psychopaths at work

It is said that 3% of the population have psychopathic characteristics. The superficial talents of psychopaths often make them successful in organisations.

The most popular recent book on the topic is *Snakes in Suits* by industrial psychologist Paul Babiak, and psychopathy expert Robert Hare, which covers the nature of **psychopaths** in organisations and explains:

- The superficial similarities (and fundamental differences) between leadership skills and psychopathic traits
- How psychopaths **manipulate** their way into work and get promoted
- The effects of their presence on colleagues and corporations.

And, because of their positions of power, it can be very difficult to expose and remove psychopaths at work.

But help is at hand, and you can find a checklist online to assess a work colleague. (The PCL-R or PCL-SV "Checklists of Psychopathy" devised by Dr. Robert Hare.) The process of removing them involves getting 360 degree evidence from colleagues and subordinates. It can be done. The first thing to do is to recognise that these people actually exist. You might think that it is **your problem** to deal with in silence. You may think it is just you that has problems with them. If you see any of the following traits, be careful, get support.

- Arrogance
- Manipulative behaviour
- Lack of guilt or remorse
- The "ABCs" of Psychopathy: No **A**nxiety; No **B**onds; No **C**onscience.

These are characteristics that a lot of us display at some time, but according to Dr Babiak the psychopath exhibits these tendencies throughout every aspect of their lives.

Stuck like glue

Babiak says: "Once they have their talons dug into a company they may be too well connected politically to shift, hiding their dangerous natures behind a network of influence and manipulation."

The difference between sociopaths and psychopaths

Psychopaths are different from sociopaths in one fundamental respect: Whereas sociopaths have no allegiance to any values or laws of wider society beyond their own small sub-group, such as a gang or cult, psychopaths have no allegiance to anything but themselves.

Both psychopaths and sociopaths are attracted to religious, non-profit, educational, legal, military and political organizations, and according to Babiak and Hare (2006), the corporate world is an increasingly "target-rich" environment for psychopaths because:

1. Some core psychopathic personality traits ("talents") may seem attractive in job applicants:

    - Assertiveness
    - Ability to appear genuine when faking sincerity
    - Ability to quickly assess vulnerabilities of people and manipulate them
    - Take-charge narcissism
    - Expertise in schmoozing and networking.

2. They may fit superficial ideas of effective "leadership" with a focus on top-down power and decision-making:

    - But with avoidance of accountability
    - Using/treating people as mere useful objects.

3. Demanding, "results-oriented" managers appear increasingly attractive to those at the top:

    - Who want power and perks but not proportionate accountability for themselves.

Knowledge is power

At home

I know a husband who keeps information from his wife. He controls all the money and pays all the bills. When his wife asks him about how much money they have, he answers with vague generalisations such as *"we have **enough**"*, *"I have transferred **some** more into my pension."*

He does what he can to limit her access to information. When he hears local gossip he deliberately does not pass it on. He openly criticises her and looks for examples of her wrongdoings.

At work

The same guy uses similar tactics to build his knowledge power at work.

Firstly, he networks well. He makes sure he spends time with people who know what is going on. He is especially good at picking up on and using the current buzz words.

He passes on information to people who can help him as a currency to be traded. With less influential people he talks in generalisations: *"production is going fine – we have enough stock"*. To suppliers, he asks for vague but popular solutions: *"we need a talent strategy"*, *"they need leadership training"*. By talking in vague generalisations he cannot be pinned down to a measurable outcome. But he can be seen to be doing something, or better still to have asked someone else to provide a solution for which they can be blamed if it is not delivered.

He searches out gossip and information about people's weaknesses. If he finds out about company plans, he keeps them to himself until the information can be traded to people he wants to impress.

He identifies who is important in his world, how they like to receive information, and what performance data they look at when assessing his performance.

He makes sure that all these key people in his world receive positive information about him in the way they like to receive it.

He makes sure that he does not get too sucked into project work that will take up valuable time for networking and impression management. He actively seeks out competent but politically naïve deputies and staff, who will work hard and deliver time-consuming projects for him so he can take the credit.

He keeps on top of performance data that he may need to influence others, but does not share unless he has to or can gain an advantage by doing so. Similarly, he holds back successes and good ideas that could benefit others, until he can gain some personal leverage from them.

He identifies what his next positions could be, and the other competitors for the jobs. He systematically collects information about key colleagues and looks for weaknesses and evidence of poor performance.

As he climbs the greasy pole he spends as much time as he can with people at the next level up. He copies what they wear, the sports and pastimes they take part in, the holiday locations they go to, the language they use and the way they speak. If he went to public school, and so did the people above him at work, then he can use this common bond to his advantage, in helping him to inhabit their world very quickly.

The culture of the organisation

He realises that to be successful in an organisation you need to build trust and rapport with the people within it, and synchronise with the real beliefs, values and culture of the organisation. For example, when he worked for a manufacturing company, with a senior management culture of English public school, where politeness and belonging are more important than performance, he was superbly polite.

Conversely, when he worked for a high tech company that was young, challenging and nerdy, he behaved as if he were Steve Jobs and wore a black turtleneck top with jeans.

When he became a bank trader, he read the real culture of the bank as risk-taking, visible personal wealth and aggressive behaviour.

Manipulative people are very good at reading the culture of the organisation, reading the people that really matter and flexing their behaviour accordingly.

We have looked at coping mechanisms for three levels of manipulation. But you can increase your effectiveness, credibility and choice in all your meetings by building your consulting skills and power.

Some of this might be copying some of the tactics of manipulative people:

- Reading people
- Flexing your behaviour
- Building trust and rapport.

But in your case, you will be doing it with authenticity, to face up to and solve real performance problems.

DON'T WORRY about appearing manipulative.

Human beings are incredibly skilled at picking up those micro signals that show you are not being authentic.

You will immediately feel the coldness if you try to use these tactics without being authentic, and they will not work.

So, always be authentic in your behaviour with the client. **That** is the first rule of consulting.

Understanding yourself

In a meeting with a client you also have another voice to listen to:

Your inner dialogue

To understand what is going on in a meeting with a client, you need to calm your internal dialogue so that you can really **hear** and see what is going on in the here and now. Anything you can do to increase your self-awareness will help you flex your behaviour to be more credible and achieve better results in your meetings.

For example, you receive an e-mail telling you that a senior client wants to talk to you about sales training.

You might have a conversation going around your head:

"Oh no, she is unhappy with the training we have done for them."

"I don't know enough about sales training – must find out more."

"I had better have some options for what we can do for them."

"We have the global sales training modules – I need to suggest them."

And when you get to meet your client your inner dialogue continues:

"Wow, I am lucky to get this time with her."

"She is so smart!"

"I must impress her with my professionalism."

"What can I say about sales training to show I know my stuff?"

So what can you do to calm your inner voice?

The fundamental principle is that the more you increase your self-awareness, the more you can:

- "Read" your clients
- See and hear and engage with your client
- Flex your behaviour
- Increase your credibility and effectiveness in the meeting.

So any tools that help you increase you self-awareness are valuable,

- Myers-Briggs
- Counselling training
- 360 degree feedback
- Transactional Analysis
- Neuro-Linguistic Programming (NLP)
- Cognitive Behavioural Therapy (CBT)
- Psychology
- Emotional Intelligence.

The more self-aware you are, and the more you are aware of others, the more power and choice in your interactions it gives you – which allows you to better manage yourself, leading to stronger relationships.

Self Management	Relationships
Flexible, open, consistent, trustworthy, authentic	Trust, balanced outlook, conflict handling, interdependence

Top tip:

- Be authentic at all times
- And see what effect it has on your clients
- They will tend to respond.

Resources

What	When
Search for a free Myers-Briggs questionnaire on the web	
Search for books on Transactional Analysis e.g. *TA and Training* by Dave Barker (1980)	
Find introductory books on NLP e.g. *Introducing NLP* by O'Connor and Seymour (1990)	
Read *CBT for Dummies* by Branch and Willson (2010) (Cognitive Behavioural Therapy) www.dummies.com	

Self-Image

Some H.R. professionals and L&D consultants will never become good Business Partners because their image of themselves holds them back.

Some see themselves as:

- **"Helpful hands"** get their affirmation from immediate external thanks and gratitude from their clients. Just do not "get" any idea of challenge as it goes against their whole construction and maintenance of their idea of self.
- **"Administrators"** and damn good at it – why would I change?
- **"Knights in shining armour"** challenge too much, too early and lock antlers. Do not spend time to build the trust and rapport.

We all behave in ways which keep ourselves consistent with our self-image. So, if my self-image is one of a helpful person, I may find it hard to ask the challenging questions required of the business partner role.

Icebergs

(We covered Thinking Traps and Icebergs in *How to be a True Business Partner*. As they are very relevant I have repeated them here.)

We often do not see reality but react to triggers that release deep emotions from our past. Reivich and Shatté (2002) have some wonderful exercises on detecting **icebergs** and **triggers** in their book *The Resilience Factor*.

Briefly, an iceberg is something in the present that releases old emotions, so that you react out of all proportion to the event. For example, your spouse might mention something about cleaning your room that triggers an outburst about your own space, which actually links back to how you were treated as a child. You may react over-negatively to people in power in your organisation if you associate their behaviour with people who had power over you in the past, for example, at school.

Reality

Triggers

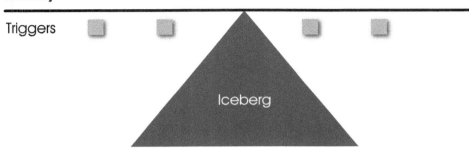

If you are reacting intensely to a situation, it could be a sign that you are being affected by an underlying belief about how the world works and how you feel the need to operate in that world, e.g. "I need to be wary of people taking advantage of me; I need to make sure I get my share."

Can you recognise any of your icebergs?

Self-awareness of icebergs and internal triggers to our emotions is an important development of emotional regulation and empathy. The more you can calm your own voices, the better you can empathise and really hear what the client is saying.

By asking open questions that challenge the client to think below the surface structure of their language, you can release underlying meanings even from very matter-of-fact answers, for example:

"How are your team doing?"

"So, they are not very effective at the moment. What do you see happening?"

"What does 'behind target' mean?"

"Which aspects of the job are they most behind with?"

This moving from surface structure of language and beliefs explains why clients can find the process very challenging and very valuable.

Another way to build your self-awareness is to become conscious of your common thinking traps.

Thinking traps

Aaron Beck, a cognitive therapist, suggested seven thinking traps that people jump into:

Jumping to conclusions	"We need to do this." ("Solutioneering")
Tunnel vision	Automatically taking short cuts and not seeing the bigger picture
Magnifying and minimising	Glass half empty/glass half full
Personalising	Attributing problems to one's own doing
Externalising	"No one can sell in this market."
Over-generalising	"That bad shot means I will never be able to do it."
Mind reading	Believing that we know what those around us are thinking

An effective consultant needs a level of self-awareness to be successful in the role. This includes recognising your own personality preferences and how you react to pressure. The more self-aware you are, the more you will be able to engage with your client; flex your style to build rapport; see the reality behind problems; and help your client face up to that reality as a trusted partner.

How to build your resilience

How you react to an event (adversity) will depend on your self-awareness, and how the event triggers your in-built triggers, beliefs and icebergs, will lead you to adopt possible thinking traps.

Hints on how to avoid thinking traps

Jumping to conclusions

Imagine that you get a message that the client wants to talk to you.

You might jump to conclusions, e.g. 😟 *"Oh no, what has gone wrong now? I wonder if the solution was delivered on time? Is she angry about xxx?"* How do you respond more resiliently?

- **Gather more data**: Spend a few minutes checking on recent deliverables to the client – is anything due? What has happened recently?
- **Talk to yourself**: "At the moment I have no evidence that this message is about anything going wrong."

If you assume that something is wrong, you won't really listen in an open-minded way when you talk to the client. But by countering your thinking trap you will be better able to be in control, ask an open question and listen carefully to what the real issue is. You will also be in a calmer state, ready to tackle any issues that come up.

Magnifying and minimising

This is about being over-positive or negative given the same information. How do you respond more resiliently?

- **Gather more data**: "What are the facts?"
- **Talk to yourself**: "Could I be over/under playing this?"

Personalising

This is about attributing problems to one's own doing, e.g. 🖐 *"That was a poor golf shot, I am useless"*, whereas your playing colleague just notices that it was a difficult downhill lie. How do you respond more resiliently?

- **Gather more data**: "Why do you think I did that?"
- **Talk to yourself**: "I am playing okay, I just didn't account for the downhill lie."

Externalising

This is the opposite of personalising, e.g. *"The wind blew it out!"* – attributing your own problems to external factors. In this way, we may protect our self-image, but may find ourselves getting angry.

How do you respond more resiliently?

- **Gather more data**: "How strong is this wind? Could it have blown it out?"
- **Talk to yourself**: "Why am I getting angry? The wind is the same for everyone, I will just have to adapt."

Over-generalising

You may think 🖐 *"I am a bad consultant"* when the facts might say otherwise. How do you respond more resiliently?

- **Gather more data**: "I will ask my clients what they value from me."
- **Talk to yourself**: "I am over-generalising from one impression."

Mind reading

You may think 😕 *"He never arrives on time, he doesn't respect me"* when perhaps he is always late for other people's meetings too. Collect further information before jumping into your trap. How do you respond more resiliently?

- **Gather more data**: "I will ask colleagues if he is always late for them and ask the client why he is late."
- **Talk to yourself**: "I do not know why he is late."

General principles for how to respond more resiliently:

- Pause
- Hold back from jumping into your trap
- Search for data
- Break the situation into Adversity Beliefs Consequences
- Ask yourself "What is real?"

> **Dave Spacey from Volvo Trucks told me:**
>
> *"My son is a pilot and he told me a similar story. After several serious accidents they found the best action initially was 'do nothing — ask the question. Which engine is on fire? Port or starboard?'"*

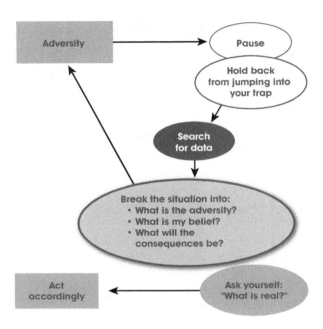

Action plan

What	When
Take a little time to reflect on your icebergs. Write them down.	
Can you think of an occasion when you reacted to adversity: In an unhelpful way? In a more resilient way?	

Ways to increase your power and influence

Sorry! There is no easy answer. The same skills that made you a good joint problem–solving consultant will improve your credibility, power and influence, mainly:

- Having a process
- Asking "clean" open questions
- Forensic listening
- Being authentic at all times
- Having self-confidence from justified achievement
- Possessing excellent technical knowledge and expertise.

Recognise that there are things you can do to build your power and influence:

- Increase your self-awareness (Myers-Briggs, etc.)
- Read more about psychology, influencing skills, etc. (See Bibliography)
- Build your qualifications
- Practise your consulting skills
- Look for feedback and coaching on your style and effectiveness in real meetings
- Keep yourself fit and healthy
- Spend time with successful people.

How do I influence people and build my credibility?

The first question is who to influence…

I suggest that you create a stakeholder map of everyone in your organisation that has influence of your career and success, e.g.

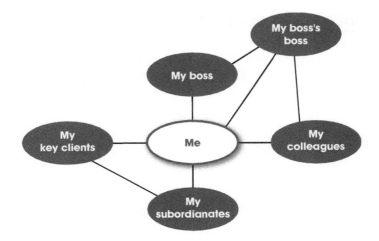

Then:

- Find out what they expect from you and what success would look like to them
- Plan how you will build your relationships with each stakeholder and deliver successes to each one in the way they like to receive information.

Forensic listening

To be really successful as an internal consultant you will have to develop your listening skills beyond the normal. This is the reason that it is normal to feel very tired after a client meeting. After all, you will have been giving the client 100% of your attention:

- Hearing every word they say
- Ensuring that you know what every acronym and word means
- Repeating back key words

- Recognising **clues** and **cues** in their language
- Probing beneath generalisations
- Formulating open questions

- Spotting micro changes in body language
- Hearing and quietening your own inner dialogue
- Keeping an eye on the time

- Making notes within your consulting process
- Using closed questions to move the client on through a process
- Controlling the conversation

- Spotting, and dealing with, psychological games, "solutioneering" and power plays.

I like the term *"forensic listening"* to describe the level of attention required. It is another level away from everyday conversation when we:

- Interrupt
- Use leading questions
- Think about what we want to say
- Ignore most of what is being said until we hear a trigger that fits with our opinion
- Wind people up
- Tell jokes
- Talk about safe "pastimes" (cars, the weather, sport)
- Keep things superficial.

In Japan you will be treated with formality and respect before you have earned the right to be treated informally. It is a bit like that in organisations.

Your first contact with senior people will be a test to see if you have the awareness and conversational skills to engage with them at a deeper level. What is this deeper level?

We covered this in *How to be a True Business Partner* but just to remind you…

Deep and surface structure meaning

Neuro Linguistic Programming (NLP) has a very useful concept of surface and deep structure of language. The world contains too much information for our brains to take in; therefore, we only select some of the millions of bits of information available. This is **DELETION**. And from this we create a simplified version. This is **DISTORTION**. And then we **GENERALISE**, so that what we say is a simplification of what we actually mean.

(Extract from *How to be a True Business Partner*)

As we move from "deep structure" to "surface structure", we generalise, change, and leave out parts of our ideas when we speak to others.

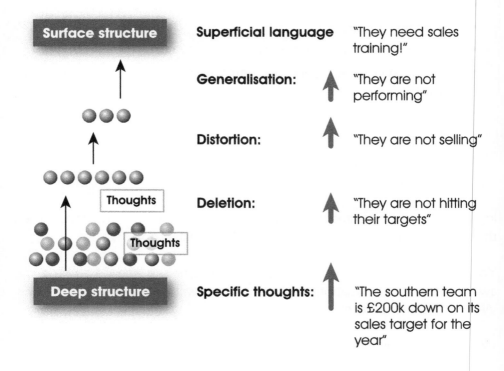

Surface structure	**Superficial language**	"They need sales training!"
	Generalisation:	"They are not performing"
	Distortion:	"They are not selling"
Thoughts	**Deletion:**	"They are not hitting their targets"
Deep structure	**Specific thoughts:**	"The southern team is £200k down on its sales target for the year"

Here are some examples of questions to move people to a deeper level:

Tactic	Surface Language	Questions
Deletion	They are not telling us what is going wrong.	Who is not telling us?
Generalisations	I can't change.	What would happen if you did?
Necessity	You must rinse it!	What would happen if you didn't?
Judgements	It is the best system for us!	Who is telling us?
Comparisons	4-4-2 is better	Than what?

Distress clues

The most valuable things I listen and watch out for are sign of distress:

- Nervous giggling and laughter
- Leaning back and making a sucking noise
- Banging the pen on the table and saying "That's the real problem!"
- Grimacing
- Frowning
- Speaking in a raised voice, e.g. "They should be doing it!"
- Parental words like "should", "ought" and "must".

If you spot one of these signs, go for it, but gently ...

Ask in a calm, soft voice:

> *"Oh, why should they be doing it?"*

Or just repeat their words and perhaps imitate their tone:

> *"You said 'they **should** be doing it!'"*

By acting as a mirror to the client, they can often learn a lot about their own problems by hearing their own words repeated.

Conversational clues

When you meet someone for the first time, you need to earn their respect and trust before they will open up to you. We often start with a superficial level of language, but include clues to greater intimacy. If you are aware and sensitive enough to spot these clues, you earn the right to move to a deeper level of meaning in your conversation.

People often stop talking when they have made an important point, to see how you will react.

For example the client says:

> *"Everything ... **seems** fine in the Stockholm office."*

If you are sensitive enough to notice a slight hesitation before "seems", and can repeat this to the client, you might unlock a deeper level of problem.

> *"Yes, it only seems okay. I am concerned about their resilience to cyber attack."*

My friend, Phil Dickinson, compares these key words or clues to *hypertext* – you click on them and it reveals a deeper level of detail.

Common clues to look out for:

- First and last words
- Doubt, concerns
- Pressure: "must!", "should!"
- String adjectives: "annoyed", "worried"
- "I", "my", "me"
- Repeating the same words.

Non verbal

- Shrugs
- Hand over mouth
- Leaning forward or backwards
- Clenched fist
- Arms folded.

We make "body pictures" of what we think and feel all the time.

In *If Only I Had Said*, Charles Margerison (2000) says:

> "People often tell us things in an oblique way. They indicate that they know or feel something but are unwilling to say more unless we pick up the clue. We should therefore expect to receive clues. We need to listen to the important words people use. They can be unusual words, words which are stressed, or just words that do not seem to relate to the situation as you see it."

People are often unsure about what they know. You need to help them see the reality of their own issues. For example, *"They need training"* is really a clue rather than an order. They are not really clear about the real problem. So when you ask *"What is happening now?"* and *"What do you want to see?"* you are helping them reveal their own problem.

By carefully listening for further clues you can reveal the real problem and the possible causes.

For example:

So what is happening now?	I feel they are **okay**.
Okay?	Yes, but I feel **uncertain** that they will hit their targets.
Uncertain?	Well, I am probably certain that they are not going to hit their targets!
What makes you think that?	They are just not accepting the new way of working **quickly enough**.
How quickly do you need them to move?	We need at least four **new format deals** in the pipeline this quarter.
How many do you have?	None!

It can be fun

But you need to give 100% attention to your client and quieten your inner dialogue.

If your personal concerns start to surface, for example, in an inappropriate leading question "*Do you think the project management course might help them?*" you can break the trust.

So quieten your internal dialogue and really listen.

One of the most common things you will start to hear in meetings is that people offer solutions before they understand the problem.

Many insecure, but macho, managers start by "solutioneering" and you will hear:

- Proposals
- Direction
- Information.

When they should still be finding out about the problem by:

- Enquiry
- Diagnosis
- Summarising.

Summarising is a great way to move a group from "solutioneering" to problem analysis, e.g.

> *"Let me just summarise what I am hearing: We have approval to build a clean area in unit 2. Can I just check - is this for all the lines in unit 2?"*

> *"Yes"*

> *"What is the current state of clean production?"*

Recognising timescales in conversations

My fellow director, Tim, used to tell me to prefix my conversations with our staff by saying *"This is what I see us doing on the next 3-5 years"*, otherwise I frightened our staff who thought I wanted change immediately.

Similarly, you need to listen to people's language to identify what timescales they are talking in. You can avoid dangerous misunderstandings by clarifying what timescales people are using. It is your job as a consultant to listen clearly and clarify where people are talking about:

Past – Present – Future

Action plan

What	When
Have you made a stakeholder map of people who have the most influence in your life?	
Pick a meeting that you are going to have and plan to deliberately improve the quality of your listening to a forensic level. Did you spot: • **Clues** and **cues** in their language. • Generalisations? • Micro changes in body language? Did you: • Quieten your own inner dialogue? • Manage to control the conversation? • Spot any psychological games, "solutioneering" and power plays?	

Permissions

"With skilled conversational control it is possible to open up a problem-solving relationship in which you give and receive permission to cross onto each other's territory to support and help."

If Only I Had Said, Charles Margerison (2000)

At the start of the meeting you will have agreed a contract and asked permission to ask questions, but this is only the start. Throughout the meeting you will be building trust and unspoken permission to challenge the client and reach new areas of intimacy. You will watch people's response carefully and recognise when they are uncomfortable and literally moving away from you. At these times, you may need to re-contact and check that your contract is still okay. Everyone has territory that they wish to protect. Your key skill will be in how you listen to people in a caring and empathetic way. It is also important to use the client's words and acronyms to show that you have really understood. It is okay to paraphrase but make sure you flag up that you are doing it.

"So, in my words I think you are... Is that correct?"

Be careful!

> *A potential client once used this "chunking down" technique on me in an interview. I felt uncomfortable and manipulated and turned down the offer of work. He had not taken time to build rapport with me and I saw his constant questioning as aggressive rather than helpful.*

So be careful:

- Build rapport first.
- Ask your questions gently.
- Watch your client's reactions.
- Give them space and time to answer.

On the other hand, it is clear from their responses that our clients are valuing this challenge the most:

- "You helped me to see it differently."
- "I hadn't thought about it like that."
- "The challenge really helped me."

This is the consulting tightrope that you walk:

- Do not challenge enough and you do not add enough value.
- Challenge too much and you may lose trust and rapport.

Clean language

One technique used in psychotherapy is to ask content free questions to encourage the client to reveal their problems through their choice of language.

In *Clean Language: Revealing Metaphors and Opening Minds* by Wendy Sullivan and Judy Rees (2008), they say:

As a Clean Language questioner:

- Listen attentively
- Ask Clean Language questions to explore a person's words, particularly their metaphors
- Listen to the answers and then ask more Clean Language questions about what they have said.

The first "Clean Language" questions they use are:

- (And) what kind of X is that?
- (And) is there anything else about X?

So far you can see that the use of language is very similar to performance consulting. The interesting new thing here is how it is used to reveal the client's **metaphors**, to understand even more about how they perceive their world.

For example, I used the metaphor **see** in the paragraph above. A client may describe their team as:

"All washed up"

"Brimming full of ideas"

"At a crossroads"

"Not knowing what road to take".

These statements are metaphorical. The team is not literally standing at a crossroads.

Metaphors allow us to think in deeper and more profound ways. They are the essence of thought. But we all have our own symbolic thinking blocks. By asking clean, open questions, listening attentively and repeating back what a client says, we can reach a profound level of shared meaning.

For example, you may say:

"So, the London sales team are the key players in this?"

(Closed question to move the client on from identifying who is involved into the performance gap analysis.)

Consultant: "How are they performing now?"

Client: "I think they are at a **crossroads**."

Consultant: "A **crossroads**? What would it be like if they were performing as you want?"

Client: "Well, they would be acting as **professional sales consultants**."

Consultant: "Do you have anyone who behaves as a professional sales consultant now?"

Client: "Yes, Stefan is highly professional, technically expert, builds trusted client relationships and brings in the big contracts."

Consultant: "If everyone thought and behaved like Stefan, what effect would that have on your sales?"

Client: "If I had a team of Stefans, we would smash the targets."

Consultant: "What would smashing them mean?"

Client: "£15 million."

Consultant: "And how much does the team standing at the crossroads bring in?"

Client: "£8 million."

Consultant: "So this performance gap could be costing us £7 million?"

[Closed question to move the client on]

Client: "Yes."

In this case the metaphors eventually crystallised into a real person, "Stefan" (the high performer). Once the desired performance could be visualised, it was a breakthrough for the client.

Finding a high performer

Finding a high performer can also have enormous benefits in the solution stage.

- How do we get everyone to perform like Stefan?
- What does Stefan do?
- How did he learn to do it?
- What knowledge does he have?
- How did he acquire the skills?

The fastest way I know to design effective performance solutions is to find a high performer and copy what they do to the rest of the target audience in the most effective way.

This is probably the key tenet of Instructional Design, but you probably knew that.

Before the meeting

So far, we have been thinking about what happens in the meeting. But what about before the meeting? After all, *"your time for choice was yesterday."*

I recently had a meeting with a very senior director from a global bank. I had been told that he was a difficult client, so I thought I had better find out something about him.

I talked to his Business Partner and asked her:

- How does he like to work?
- Is he big picture or detailed?
- Is he head or heart?
- Where did he work before?
- Where will the meeting be held?
- How long have we arranged the meeting to be?
- What is he expecting from the meeting?

Then I Googled him and downloaded a picture of him talking at a conference.

Following this I sent him an e-mail introducing myself, my background, qualifications and website and clarified the purpose of the meeting, the time available and the location.

I then made sure that I dressed in similar business dress to him; arrived at the meeting room early; prepared the chairs so that he was invited to sit on my right; put a copy of his conference photo on the desk.

When he arrived I looked in him the eye, mirrored his posture and shook his hand with a firm handshake. The start of the meeting was around the fact that I had a photo of him that I had downloaded from Google. We then got on to common people we knew from his previous company ... by now we were off on the right foot.

The more you can prepare for a meeting the better.

A simple checklist

Before the meeting check:

- When is the meeting?
- How long do we have?
- Who will be there?
- Where is it?
- What are the stated objectives?

Summary

You can build your consulting power in a number of ways:

- Listen to and quieten your *inner dialogue* ☯ .
- **Be authentic at all times, and see what effect it has on your clients — they will tend to respond positively.**
- Be aware of your thinking traps and **how you react to an adversity**.
- Draw your own **system diagram** of the people you need to influence.
- Practise **forensic listening** to get closer to the meanings behind superficial language.
- Watch out for distress cues and conversational clues.
- Be aware of **timescales** in people's language.
- **Use "clean" questions** (short open questions) so the client can project their meaning onto the question.
- Listen for and repeat **metaphors**.
- **Find high performers** and use them to visualise the high performance.
- Use the time before a meeting to prepare for success.

5   Power and Politics - Advice to a new CEO

Dear friend,

This is my advice to you based on the best article I know on "Power and Politics in Organizational Life" by Abraham Zalenick in 1971. All quotes are from him and I have tried to keep the flavour of his wonderful article.

*Don't be mislead into thinking that your organisation is a purely rational place. They are **political structures,** they operate by distributing authority for the exercise of power.*

*Human beings tend to make **comparisons** as a basis of self esteem. Organisations are pyramids, producing a scarcity of positions the higher one moves up the hierarchy. People **compete** for power in an economy of **scarcity**.*

Whilst appointment to positions comes from above, affirmation of position comes from below. Subordinates can withdraw affirmation and support, giving them constituency power – so look after your constituencies as well as your boss's.

Build your power base through:

- *The quantity of **formal authority** in the role*

- *You reputation for **competence***

- *The attractiveness of your **personality** (respect and liking).*

The ability to use your power depends on the total esteem with which others regard you.

Don't confuse compliance with commitment. Compliance can be a tactic to avoid changes and commitment. In the power relations among executives, the so-called areas of common interest are usually reserved for the banalities of human relationships. The more significant areas of attention usually force conflict on interests, especially competition for power, to the surface.

You need to be able to handle this competition — it is inevitable.

Conflicts for resources are usually worked out through bargaining. However, with power issues there are no objective measures of right and wrong here, and the key question is "Who gets power and position?". Organisations are political structures which feed on the psychology of comparison.

Don't be misled by your organisation's rituals around participation, democracy and power sharing — the real outcome is the consolidation of power around a central figure to whom other individuals make emotional attachments.

If you fail to deliver what the constituency demands, they may form a new coalition and look for a better power figure to follow.

Individuals remain vulnerable to their own blind spots and unconscious reactions to striving for power.

Watch out for rituals and ceremonies

Power can become ritualised and rigid. Structures, procedures and other ceremonies emerge to create the illusion of solving problems, but in reality only give people something to discharge valuable energies on, e.g. bringing people together in a committee on the naïve grounds that the exchange of ideas is bound to produce a solution.

Superiors and subordinates in any power structure are constantly tempted to manipulate each other as a way of gaining control over one's environment, and the more so when there is a lack of confidence and credibility in the organisation's efforts to solve problems in realistic ways.

When the heads of organisations are unsure of their power, they become defensive or fail to understand the structure and potential of power coalitions. The easy solution is to play for time by invoking rituals which may temporarily reduce anxiety.

Do not despair — you reached your position of power through competence and the ability to face and solve real problems. This is what will keep you in power. One of your main jobs is to bring similarly talented individuals into positions for the legitimate use of power, to counter the irrational problem avoidance collusion in the organisation and the natural tendency to revert to defence mechanisms and ritual by less competent and fading leaders.

*(Abraham Zalenick thinks the most effective leaders **take a problem-solving approach**).*

Use a rational problem-solving process on all issues and be wary of the inevitability of people using politics and energy to avoid solving problems but to protect their power.

What does this mean for performance consulting?

I am convinced that with the right:

- Stakeholders and power holders in a room
- Systematic approach to problem-solving
- Neutral and skilled facilitator

… one can resolve any organisational problem.

But we have to recognise that the irrational, emotional and power-ridden nature of all organisations means that this is a rare event. Internal consultants such as L&D, H.R. and I.T. operate within the "reality" of their organisation "box". Internal consultants need to develop their:

- Power base
- Influence and credibility
- Personal skills
- Resilience.

The emotional power, rituals and defence mechanisms in their organisations may actually oppose rational problem-solving for the benefit of the organisation.

Final Summary

We have added some more stages to the 7-step performance consulting process.

Firstly – anything you can do to **build your self-awareness** gives you more power and flexibility in your client meetings.

Secondly – the time **before the meeting** is critical for planning and gaining intelligence about the client and how they prefer to work.

Then – if you are in the meeting and you lose trust:

If it is | Innocent manipulation | continue with trust and use the Performance Consulting process and your consulting skills to avoid "solutioneering" and help the client to face up to the real business problem.

| Client resists by using power |

Recognise that you are in a negotiation – work out your power and **negotiate**.

| Dealing with real manipulation |

If you meet someone with no conscience and power: do something different, break the pattern, check if they are a psychopath, get out of there (start looking for another job).

So, that's all Folks!

I hope this book will increase your awareness of what is going on around you in your "real" organisation.

You need to be aware of the use of power and manipulation.

Most of the time an authentic, problem-solving approach will work with most of your clients. But when it doesn't, I hope the advice in this book will help you to:

- Have more choice about your behaviour
- Build your credibility and effectiveness in your consulting role.

And remember, the first rule of consulting is to be authentic at all times.

> *I am sending you out as sheep in the midst of wolves, so be wise as serpents and innocent as doves. (Matthew 10:16, The Bible)*

I would love to hear your stories and feedback.

Regards

Nigel Harrison

This book is the third in a series on Performance Consulting.

1. Harrison, N. (2000) *Improving Employee Performance* (Kogan Page). Now available as a download at www.performconsult.co.uk

2. Harrison, N. (2008) *How to be a True Business Partner by Performance Consulting* available from Amazon or www.performconsult.co.uk.

Blog: www.performanceconsultingbook.co.uk

Contact the author: nigel@performconsult.co.uk

Babiak, P. and Hare, R.D. (2006) *Snakes in Suits: When Psychopaths Go to Work* (New York: Regan Books).

Barker, D. (1980) *TA and Training* (Hampshire: Gower Press).

Berne, E. (1964) *Games People Play: The Psychology of Human Relationships* (Harmondsworth: Penguin Books).

Block, P. (1981) *Flawless Consulting* (Erlanger, KY: Pfeiffer & Co).

Bibliography

Branch, R. and Willson, R. (2010) *Cognitive Behavioural Therapy for Dummies* (Chichester, UK: Wiley).

Charvet, S.R. (1997) *The Words that Change Minds, 2nd edn* (Dubuque, Iowa: Kendall/Hunt).

ESRC (2006) *Research and Management,* 18 May.

Guenole, N. (2013) *Maladaptive Personality at Work: Exploring the Darkness* (London: Goldsmiths, University of London).

Gilbert, T.F (1978) *Human Competence: Engineering Worthy Performance* (New York: McGraw Hill).

Harrison, N. (2008) *How to be a True Business partner by Performance Consulting* (Sheffield, UK: Nigel Harrison).

Mager, R.F. and Pipe, P. (1970) *Analysing Performance Problems* (Belmont, CA: Fearon).

Maister, D. (2003) *Managing the Professional Services Firm* (UK: Simon and Schuster).

Margerison, C.J. (2000) *If Only I Had Said* (London: Management Books).

Peters, S. (2012) *The Chimp Paradox* (London: Vermilion).

O'Connor, J. and Seymour, J. (1990) *Introducing NLP* (London: Mandala).

Rackham, N. and Carlisle, J. (1978) *The behaviour of successful negotiators. Journal of European Industrial Training,* 2(6), pp. 6–11.

Reivich, K. and Shatté, A. (2002) *The Resilience Factor – 7 Keys to Finding your Inner Strengths and Overcoming Life's Hurdles* (Chicago, IL: Broadway Books).

Robertson, I.H. (2013) *The Psychologist,* March.

Robinson, D.G. and Robinson, J.C. (1995) *Performance Consulting* (San Francisco, CA: Berret-Koehler).

Sullivan, W, and Rees, J. (2008) *Clean Language: Revealing Metaphors and Opening Minds* (UK: Crown House).

The Arbinger Institute (2002) *Leadership and self-deception: getting out of the box* (San Francisco, CA: Berret-Koehler).

The Bible, Matthew 10:16. English Standard Version 2001.

The Psychologist (2013) March.

Tieger, P. and Barron-Tieger, B. (1998) *The Art of Speed Reading People* (Palo Alto, CA: Little Brown).

Tzu Sun (1963) *The Art of War. China 500 BC*. Translated by S. Griffith (USA: Oxford University).

Zaleznik, A. (1971) *Power and Politics in Organisational Life* (New York: Harvard University Press).

The end

Reflect on what you have just read. How does it relate to your experience?

Notes

Notes

How to be a True Business Partner
by Performance Consulting

performance consulting : uk

This book is about what really matters as an effective business partner or performance consultant.

Chartered Psychologist, Nigel Harrison has over twenty years experience in solving organisational performance problems and training internal consultants to be effective in their role.

The book includes a simple 7-step consulting process and covers real issues such as:
- What does it mean to be a business partner?
- Dealing with power and manipulation.
- Staying resilient and how to turn ideas into action.

By following the guidance in this book any business partner will be able to build better rapport with their clients, help them face up to their real problems, quantify performance gaps and justify any investment in solutions. When you can do all this you can start to become a true business partner.

Sample contents

What does it mean to be a business partner?
Fantasy and reality in organisations
What sort of relationship do our clients really want?

The Resilient Consultant
Business partner attributes
Building your resilience to overcome setbacks
Hints on how to avoid thinking traps

Thinking of the 7-step process in a new way
Building trust and rapport
What happens when you do not trust your client?
Coping with game playing and manipulation
Power play – negotiation

Facing up to the problem
Deep and surface structure meaning
Bouncing between negative and positive

Building powerful solutions
How to turn an idea into action
Drawing stakeholder maps

> *"A really good read, goes into the tricks of the trade..."*
>
> Allan Watkinson
> – Competency Manager, Reuters IS

Purchase from:
http://www.performanceconsultingbook.co.uk/products-page/